Making Masks

**CRAFT AND
DESIGN**

Making Masks

by

G C Payne

PELHAM BOOKS

First published in Great Britain by
Pelham Books Ltd
52 Bedford Square
London WC1B 3EF
1978

ISBN 0 7207 0988 1

Filmset and printed photolitho by
Ebenezer Baylis and Son Ltd.,
The Trinity Press, Worcester, and London,
and bound by Dorstel Press, Harlow

Contents

6

Introduction

What do you think of when you hear the word "mask"?

The mask a burglar wears when he wants to hide his face during a robbery?

The masks worn at Hallowe'en to give people a fright?

These are two of the ways in which masks are worn today, but the story of masks goes back into history a very long way for they have been made and used by people all over the world for many different purposes.

Whatever the reason for making a mask, it seems to change the person who wears it. It not only makes the wearer look different, it makes him feel different too. Have you ever worn a mask? Did you notice how you immediately seemed to take on a different character — the mask's character — and do what the mask told you to do?

This book will show you a number of ways of making masks: some very simple, needing little time or skill to make and others needing a good deal of care and attention. But first, let us look at some of the reasons people have had for making masks, and how they have used them. Then we can start thinking about making and using them ourselves. This is important. Masks should be used and you will find that you get better ideas and results when you make a mask with a definite purpose in mind.

Many masks were made for use in battle. In some tribes the warriors painted masks directly on to their faces and even over the whole of their bodies to make themselves look fiercer and more frightening. Sometimes a great ceremony was made of this putting on of war paint, to help the warriors feel braver and stronger and more ready to go into battle.

Medieval knights and Japanese warriors wore very elaborate helmets for fighting in. These were originally designed to protect the soldiers from swords and lances, but they were developed to make him look more imposing and to strike terror into the enemy. They were not only used in battle. When the army was on parade, the helmets gave the soldiers a much more splendid appearance. Sometimes special masks or helmets were made for parades. These were too heavy and complicated to wear in battle but they made the warriors feel and look much more imposing when they were on display.

Oxygen masks and the helmets worn by aircraft and tank crews are today's version of the battle mask, but of course they are for protection only and are rarely seen by the enemy. Nevertheless they do have an effect on the men who wear them.

Many masks were made for religious reasons. People as far apart as Eskimos, New Guinea head hunters and the Red Indians of North America, all made masks which were used in religious ceremonies. Sometimes these masks were kept very secret and only certain members of the tribe were allowed to see them. At special times of the year, when ceremonies and dances were performed in honour of their gods, selected members, almost always men, wore them and the people of the village saw their fellow tribesmen, transformed into animals, spirits or demons, parading and dancing in the flickering, hallucinatory glow of the fire. It must have been an extraordinary experience, both for the performers and for those who watched.

Very often, only one or two people in the tribe were allowed to make masks. Only they were allowed to gather the materials: wood, feathers, bone and fur, and fashion them into masks which were made according to secret rules passed down from father to son for hundreds of years.

Masks were also used in dances and rituals performed to bring good luck to the tribe's hunting and fishing expeditions. Some tribesmen would play the part of the hunter while other masked dancers would imitate the behaviour and movements of the hunted creatures. These ceremonies were a vital part of the people's lives as their survival depended on the success of the hunters.

Some of these rituals were very complicated and the boys who were to take part in them had to spend a long time learning how to wear the masks, which often had moving parts operated by strings and levers, and how to imitate the creatures they were going to represent. Some learnt their parts so well that when the performance took place, accompanied by music and chanting, they actually seemed to the watchers to become the animals, birds or fishes whose behaviour they had studied for so long.

Some of these masks, collected by explorers from tribes all over the world, can now be seen in museums. But no mask was made just to be put on show: it was a

symbol of a deep religious belief and was meant to be worn as part of a tribe's life and tradition. Many people, among them painters and sculptors such as Picasso and Henry Moore, have considered these masks to be very powerful works of art and they have had a great influence on the work of some of today's most famous artists.

Masks had a role to play in medicine, too. Both the Red Indian medicine man and the African witch doctor used them as an important part of their treatment. The changed appearance of the doctor, heavily disguised in an elaborate mask and costume, made the patient and his relatives believe that he was being treated not by an ordinary man but by a supernatural being with special powers and sometimes this belief really did help to effect a cure.

The "devil dancers" of Ceylon, who were called in to cure people suffering from all sorts of diseases, wore special masks for each type of illness they were asked to cure. They had different masks for the treatment of fevers, blindness, deformities, even stammering; they all portrayed the trouble they were intended to cure.

Surgeons in operating theatres today still wear masks, although their purpose is quite different, being simply intended to prevent infection. Nevertheless, the appearance of the people wearing them does change: the blankness of the mask makes them look impassive and dehumanised.

In western theatre today, actors wear make-up to help them take on the character they are playing and to make them easily identifiable in the bright stage lighting. In many types of theatre in other parts of the world, the type of make-up used and how it is put on to define character follows a much more rigid set of conventions. The Greek and Roman theatres of over two thousand years ago used masks with a particular pattern to identify specific characters and the Japanese "Noh" plays require masked characters as did the "Topeng" dramatic performances of the nineteenth century in Java. There are many other examples of the use of masks in the theatre — perhaps the most familiar is the special make-up, wigs and clothing that clowns in the circus wear, to show what sort of clown they are.

There are also, of course, masks worn just for fun, like the Hallowe'en ones we mentioned at the beginning. Have you ever seen the carnival "Big Heads" worn in parades and at festivals? Masked balls were especially popular in the eighteenth century. Well-known people could go to a ball and "let their hair down" while wearing a mask, knowing that nobody could recognise them and be shocked.

So you can see that the story of masks is long and very interesting. Perhaps as you try out some of the different ways of making masks explained in this book, you will want to find out more about them and the many roles they have played in people's lives.

Card Masks – Flat

Only simple materials and equipment are needed to make really effective flat card masks. They can be varied in shape: try basing them on birds or butterflies (see colour plate 1, facing page 12) or any other shape you fancy.

Fig. 1

EYE MASKS

You will need:

A piece of card — from a cardboard box, such as a cereal packet

Craft knife and a firm cutting board or a pair of scissors

Pencil

Paintbrush

Paint — poster or powder paint, or acrylic or emulsion paint (if you use the last two, wash all brushes immediately after use and be careful to protect your clothes)

Glue — PVA medium is good: it becomes transparent as it dries and leaves little trace; it will hold paper, card, plastic, wood and most other materials firmly and sets quickly so that work can go on without having to stop for it to dry.

To make sure that the two sides of the mask look exactly the same: first score a line down the centre of the card, using the back of a scissor blade.

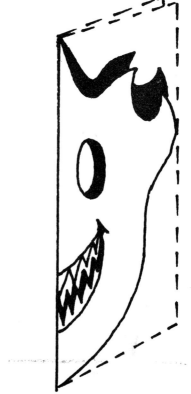

Fig. 2

Fold card in half and draw half the mask onto the folded card (Fig. 1), making sure that the middle of the mask is at the fold. Cut while it is still folded, through both thicknesses of card (Fig. 2).

Painting

Whatever sort of paint you use, make sure it is dense and thick to give strong clear colours. Watery paint will produce a very disappointing result.

The painting of your mask is very important and needs careful thought. Try to make your painted shapes echo the shapes of the outline and eye holes (see Figs. 3–5) so that they combine to give a complete effect.

Fig. 3

Fig. 4

Fig. 5

11

Use both dark and light colours for contrast but do not combine too many very bright colours or they will clash.

The masks in colour plate 1 are painted in just one colour (metallic paints are very effective used like this) and completed with patterns of beads, sequins or buttons. Make sure you use a strong adhesive such as PVA medium to attach them.

Folded card mask

Fixing the mask

To keep the mask on your head use flat elastic. Either staple it to the back of the mask or thread it through holes punched at either side, knotting the ends at the back so they do not show.

These masks can also be mounted on sticks and simply held in front of your eyes.

FACE MASKS

The same method can be used to make masks which cover the whole of your face. Figs. 6 and 7 show what unusual, exotic shapes these can take. Do not just copy

Fig. 6

Fig. 7

1. (*Above left*) Card eye masks decorated with sequins and beads

2. (*Above right*) Mask made of card and scrap materials

3. Paper plate mask with card decorations

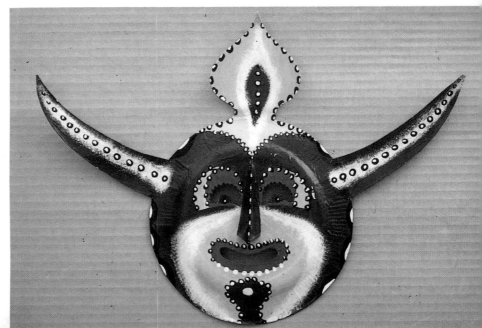

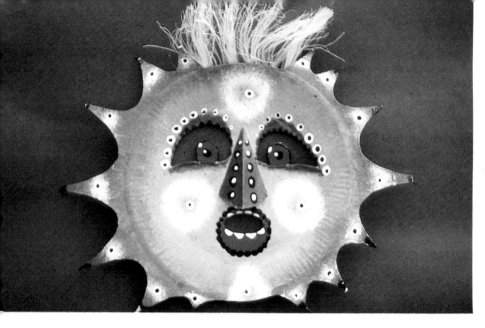

4. Paper plate mask

5. (*Below left*) Card tube mask with pasta decoration

6. (*Below right*) Casting from a plastic container with card decorations and features

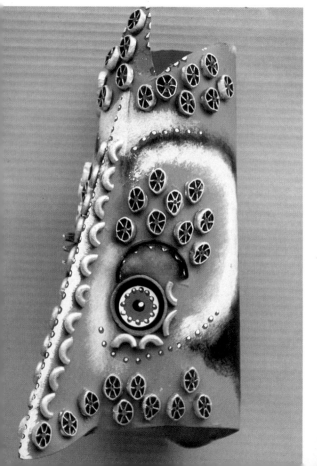

7. Mask based on laminated paper balloon casting

8. (*Below left*) Helmet mask made from card cylinders and ball casting

9. (*Below right*) Helmet mask

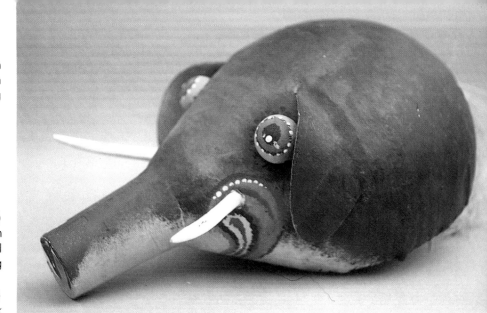

10. (*Above left*)
Folded card mask

11. (*Above right*)
Card and string mask
covered with cooking
foil

12. Folded card mask

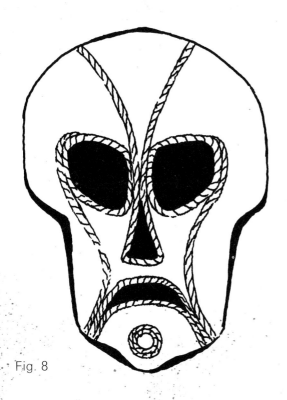

Fig. 8

Features can also be made of card. Fig. 9 shows a choice of noses for a card mask. Which do you think is most suitable? Make a few different ones and try them on your mask. Colour plates 10 and 12 (opposite) show face masks with folded card noses.

A collection of scrap materials: buttons, beads, egg-boxes, plastic containers etc., is very useful for making features and decorations for masks; colour plate 2

the shape of real faces; be inventive and fanciful, experiment with different shapes to create masks which are cheerful, ferocious, sad, anxious or whatever you like.

Features

Fig. 8 shows how to outline eyes, mouth etc. with string, stuck on with PVA medium; colour plate 11 (opposite) shows a similar mask covered with aluminium cooking foil and black shoe polish.

Fig. 9

(facing page 12) shows how effective some of these can be.

Use PVA medium to stick them in place. Mixed with water, it also makes a good varnish for masks. It gives them a glossy finish, protects the paint and makes them last much longer.

PAPER PLATE MASKS

Paper plates, usually thrown away after use, can be salvaged, cleaned and made into very attractive masks. Have them bulging either backwards or forwards to get the effect you want.

Fig. 10 shows how pieces of card can be stuck on them to make more interesting shapes; colour plates 3 (facing page 12) and 4 (between pages 12 and 13) show finished paper plate masks; these were decorated with card shapes and scrap materials, then painted with emulsion paint and varnished with PVA medium.

Fig. 10

Card Masks – Three Dimensional

Cardboard can be used to make three-dimensional masks which either fit right over your head and rest on your shoulders, or sit like a hat on top of your head. Both can be worn with a costume to cover your body completely and if you make the hat type it will make you seem much taller.

The easiest way to make one of these masks is to choose a cardboard box of the right size, simply add features and decorations and paint it, but you will be able to make a much more individual mask if you start with a flat piece of card.

You will need:

A piece of card – stiff enough to keep its shape but also capable of being bent into a smooth curve
Craft knife or scissors
Pencil
Staples or adhesive – PVA medium is good
Wallpaper paste – use a small amount of powder from a sachet and mix to a smooth paste, following the instructions on the packet
Paste brush

Cut card into the right size rectangle, according to whether you want it to fit over your head or rest on top of it, then draw a line down the centre as shown in Fig. 11.

Card tube mask with pasta decoration

Fig. 11

Cut out eyes and mouth — make sure that they are in the right places for you to see and speak through if it is to go over your head — then bend it round into a cylinder (Fig. 12) or a cone (Fig. 13). Join the ends with staples or adhesive.

Cut top and bottom edges into the shapes you want, as shown in figures.

Features

Features can be built up with card or scrap materials such as plastic cups and pasta covered with metallic paint (see colour plate 5 between pages 12 and 13).

Fix large card features in place with strips of paper. Paste these over the joins with wallpaper paste or PVA medium as in Fig. 13. This will strengthen the joins, give a smoother effect and get rid of gaps.

As the inside surface of a mask like this will be seen when you wear it, you could paint it with a contrasting colour or with black.

Fig. 12

Fig. 13

Fig. 14

Fig. 15

16

Masks Made On Buckets, Balls And Balloons

These masks are made of a shell of laminated paper on to which features and decorations in card, scrap materials etc. can be built. Laminated paper is easily made by pasting layers of absorbent paper, such as newspaper, on top of each other. In order to build these layers into a shape suitable for a mask you need a support to hold them in shape while they dry and become rigid.

Paper mask made on a plastic container

MAKING THE LAMINATED SHELL

You will need:

A support — Figs. 16–19 show some of the things that can be used. Flexible objects with smooth surfaces are most suitable, so look for some conveniently sized plastic or rubber things such as a bucket, a bowl, a plastic ice-cream container, a ball or a balloon.

Newspaper

Scissors

Paste — cold water paste, cellulose paste or PVA medium are all suitable and should be mixed to a consistency that will soak into the paper without being runny.

Cold water paste and cellulose paste will produce hard, rigid shapes while PVA will produce flexible shapes. But water colour paints will not take on a surface made with PVA medium unless more medium is mixed with the paint.

Paste brush

Liquid soap or Vaseline

Balls and balloons tend to be difficult to control as you are working, so hang balloons on strings (Fig. 20) and hold balls and balloons in a plastic bowl (Fig. 21).

Smear the surface of the support with liquid soap or Vaseline so that the paper

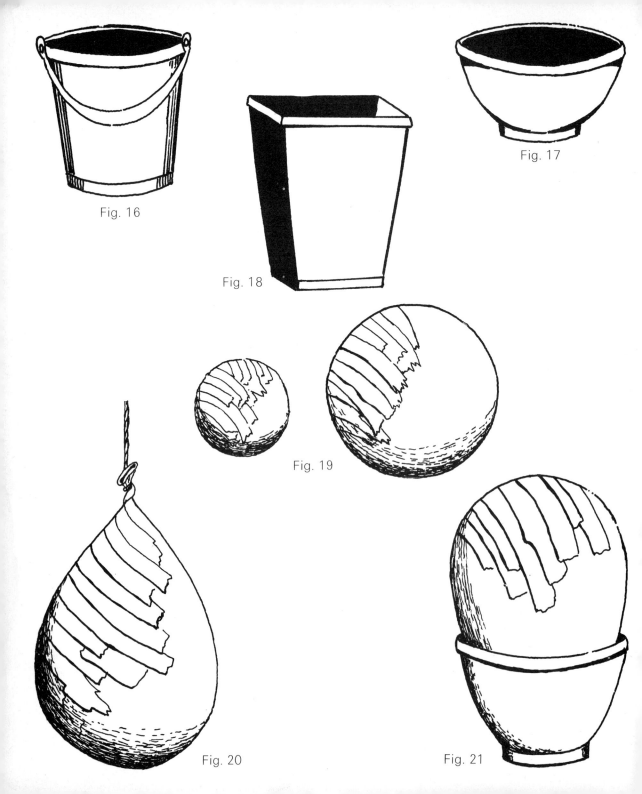

Fig. 16

Fig. 17

Fig. 18

Fig. 19

Fig. 20

Fig. 21

will come away from the support easily when dry.

Tear newspaper into strips 2–3cm (1–1½in) wide (on small objects or sharply curved surfaces they should be narrower).

Sometimes you may only need to cover half a bucket or ball to get the shape you want for a mask. Decide how much of the surface you are going to cover before you start putting on the paper.

Leave a small area round the valve of a balloon uncovered so that the balloon can be removed later.

With a wide brush, put a generous layer of paste onto the surface of the support and begin to smooth strips of paper onto it with the brush. Let the strips overlap each other slightly (see Figs. 19–21) to make a stronger shape, and have all the strips

Paper mask made on a plastic bucket

running in the same direction. This will show you when each layer is completed.

Try to keep a smooth surface, avoiding wrinkles and air bubbles — use your fingers to keep the paper lying perfectly flat.

Always use plenty of paste and make sure that it has soaked right into the paper as this will give strength to the finished shape.

Depending on the size of the mask, paste on between 4 and 6 complete layers of strips. For a balloon about the size of your head, or a 2 gallon bucket, 4 layers will suffice. Increase the number of layers only if the shape is larger or if you want the finished mask to be particularly strong, but remember that more layers will make the mask heavier and more uncomfortable to wear.

When you have finished, leave the whole thing to dry.

Drying

Hang balloons up with string and put balls to dry in a basin, making sure that as little of the pasted paper as possible touches the rim. Plastic buckets etc. will probably be safest turned upside down while the paper layers dry.

It is best to dry the shapes in a warm place, especially balloons, for if it is cold the air inside will contract and this will produce unsightly and difficult-to-paint wrinkles on the surface of the paper. But do not try to force-dry them over a radiator or near a fire, for this will make the air inside expand and split the paper covering or even burst the balloon.

Drying will usually take 2–3 days in a warm room and as they dry the layers of paper will harden.

When it is dry and hard, pull the paper shell off buckets and bowls. If you have gone all round a bucket, make a vertical cut in the paper in order to remove it. To join the two halves again, stick a few strips of paper over both the inside and the outside of the cut.

Similarly, if you have completely covered a ball, make a cut right round it at the widest part, being careful to cut through only the paper, not the ball. The two halves

Fish mask from a balloon casting

can then be pulled off separately and either used singly or joined together with pasted paper strips to remake the sphere.

Balloons may be left inside the shape or removed by untying the knot to deflate the balloon. It can then be taken out and possibly used again. If the valve is in the way but you cannot undo the knot, prick the balloon and cut off the valve. Cover the hole left in the paper shell with pasted paper strips if your design for the mask requires it, and allow them to dry and harden.

TURNING THE LAMINATED SHELLS INTO MASKS

Figs. 22-25 show how scrap card and other waste materials, stuck on with wallpaper paste or PVA medium, can provide features and decoration and turn

Bird mask from a balloon casting

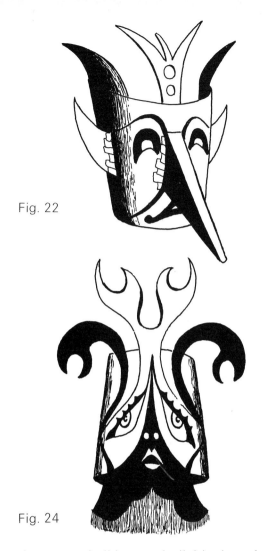

Fig. 22

Fig. 24

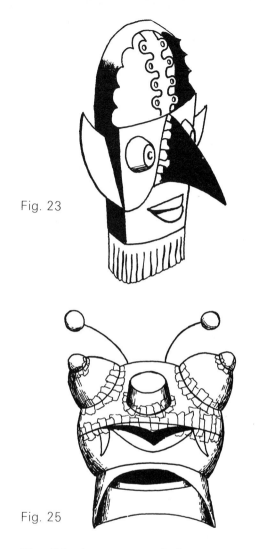

Fig. 23

Fig. 25

the paper shell into an individual mask.

It is helpful to hold features, especially larger ones, temporarily in place with dressmaker's pins while the glue dries. These can be removed once the feature is set in place.

Figs. 22 and 23 are face masks made from a shape which covered half a bucket.

Fig. 24 shows a mask from a complete bucket casting (paper shell) and colour plate 6 (between pages 12 and 13) shows one made on a square plastic container.

You can also make a mask by grouping together several castings of different sizes, made on different-sized balls for example, as in Fig. 25.

Adding card cylinders to castings made on large plastic balls can produce masks that look rather like helmets (see Figs. 26–29). Glue card cylinders inside the castings with PVA medium and if necessary

Fig. 27

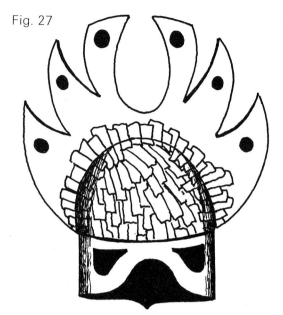

Fig. 26

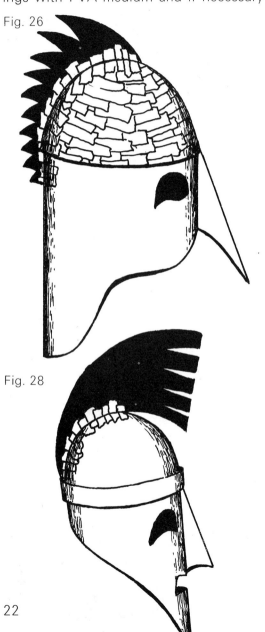

Fig. 29

Fig. 28

secure them with pasted paper strips or a band of card as in Fig. 28. Colour plates 8 and 9 (between pages 12 and 13) are of helmet masks made like this. Notice the use of scrap materials to complete the masks and add interest.

CUTTING AND DECORATING BALLOON CASTINGS

If you have made a balloon casting, look at its shape carefully from all angles to see what ideas for masks you can get from it. Depending on its shape and size, a balloon casting may be cut in several ways to produce quite different shapes which can be worn in a variety of positions.

Figs. 30–33 illustrate different ways of cutting balloon castings. Do not throw

Paper mask made from several balloon castings

Fig. 30

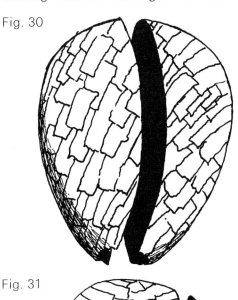

Fig. 31

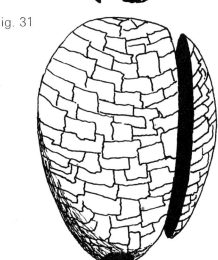

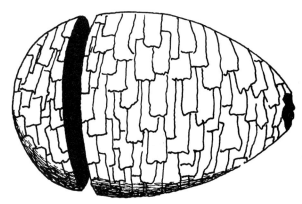

Fig. 32

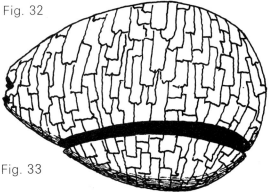

Fig. 33

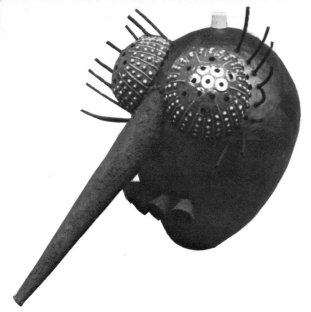

Fantasy mask made from balloon and ball castings

Fig. 34

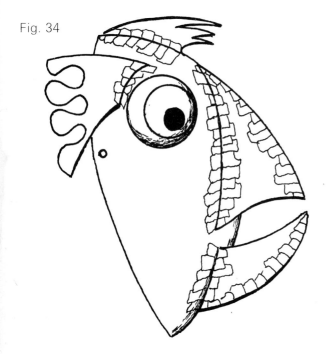

away the smaller pieces you cut off. These can be used for making such features as ears or horns and sometimes even another, smaller mask as in colour plate 23 (facing page 37).

Figs. 34–38 show how balloon castings can be developed into masks of very different characters, according to how they are cut and what features they are given with the help of card, plastic cups, egg-boxes, string etc. (See also colour plate 7 between pages 12 and 13.)

Masks made in this way are very light, in spite of the fact that they can be quite large, so they are comfortable to wear for long periods, in a play for example, and do not hamper movement if they are worn in a dance.

Fitting the masks

The way to keep the masks on your head will vary according to their shape and how you are going to wear them. Usually a single strip of flat elastic passed through holes in the sides and knotted at the back, or ribbons, similarly attached and tied behind the head or under the chin will be sufficient.

Fig. 35 shows an alternative. Sew a piece of cloth onto the mask and tie the corners under the chin to keep it firmly in place. With the mask in position, mark eye holes to see through. Remove it from your face and cut them out with a craft knife. Large holes are often not necessary, so make them small to begin with and only enlarge them if your vision is too restricted.

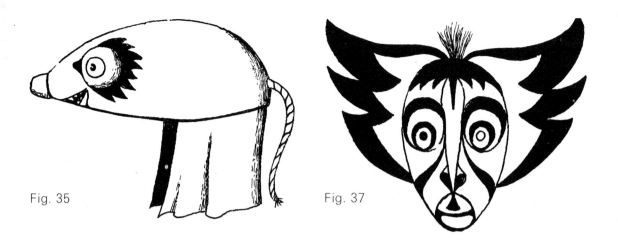

Fig. 35

Fig. 37

Fig. 36

Fig. 38

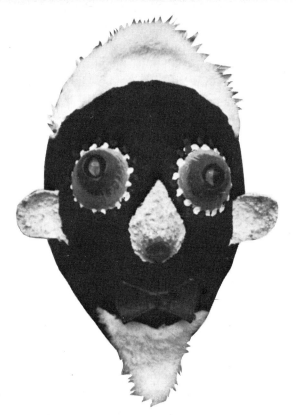

Mask made from waste section
of balloon casting

With some shapes of mask it may be
necessary to make an extra hole in an
unobtrusive place so that you can breathe
easily. This is important if you are going to
move about a lot while wearing the mask.
It will also help to keep you cool inside it.

Another interesting way of mask-making
on a balloon is shown in colour plate 16
(between pages 36 and 37). String soaked
in plaster of Paris was wound round a
balloon to form a network. After this had
dried well it was cut off the balloon in two
halves and each part turned into a mask
with features of balsa wood, plastic
scraps, etc. After painting, the whole mask
was given a coating of PVA medium,
inside and outside. This prevents the
plaster cracking and breaking off in flakes
and gives the mask a certain amount of
flexibility.

Painting

Much of the effect of these masks will
depend on how they are painted. Think of
the mask as a whole as you work out
patterns and shapes in colour so that they
fit in with the basic shape, the features you
have added and the character you want to
give your mask. The drawings and photo-
graphs throughout this book will perhaps
give you ideas of how to do this.

This method of casting masks offers
endless possibilities. If you use your
imagination and are ready to experiment,
you will find all sorts of ways to bring your
ideas to life.

Masks Made On Clay Moulds

One disadvantage with the masks described in the previous section — those built on buckets, balls and balloons — is that you have no control over the basic shape, which is dictated by the shape of whatever object you have used as a support for the paper casting. Also, the casting as it comes off the mould is quite featureless and everything needed to give the mask a character has to be added later.

To build features into the basic shape of the mask, you must use a quite different sort of support. You will need either the modelling clay used for making pots and models, which goes hard when left exposed to the air, or Plasticine, which does not harden though it remains firm enough to keep its shape if paper laminations are made on it.

Both have advantages and disadvantages. Modelling clay is cheap, so that quite large models can be made at no great expense and as it sets hard the same mould can be used several times. However, once it has hardened it does need to be mixed with water again and worked to make it pliable before it can be re-used. It can also be very messy if care is not taken when working with it, and it shrinks as it dries, so allowance must be made for this when working out the size of the mould.

Plasticine is expensive, but it is clean to use and does not require reworking in

Clay mould for face mask

order to use it over and over again as it remains plastic (flexible). It is sometimes difficult to remove a paper mask from a Plasticine mould without damaging the original modelling, so it is not so suitable for making a series of identical masks. You will have to decide which of these clays to use according to your particular purpose.

MAKING THE MOULD

You will need:

Clay or Plasticine
Modelling board
Paper — to make a template (pattern) for the mould
Pencil
Scissors

Elaborate modelling tools are not necessary; your fingers can do all that is required.

First work out the size you want your mould to be, remembering to make allowance for the fact that modelling clay will shrink by about one-sixth as it dries.

It is a good idea to draw the outline you want for the mould on a piece of paper, cut it out and place it on the modelling board. Then you can make your mould actually on the paper to exactly the size and shape you want. The paper will also help to prevent the clay sticking to the board, which might cause it to crack as it dries.

Modelling

Figs. 39–41 show the steps in making a mould for a face mask.

Fig. 39: Model the basic shape, concentrating on making it to the correct size, shape and depth of clay. *It is important that there should be no undercuts* which make it very difficult to take the finished casting off the mould. Section A, showing the shape you would see if you cut the clay between the arrows, illustrates how the

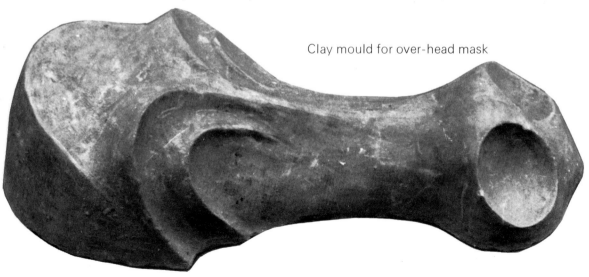

Clay mould for over-head mask

28

Fig. 39

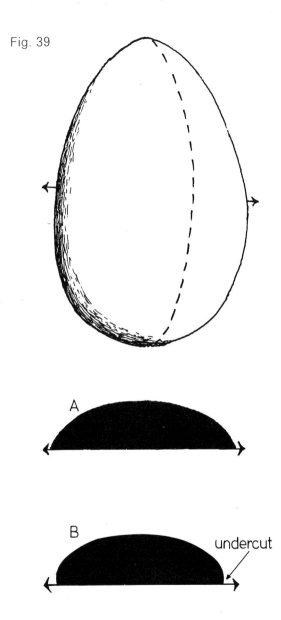

A

B

undercut

Fig. 40

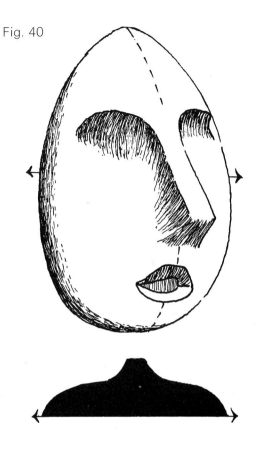

clay should be modelled to avoid under-cuts. Section B illustrates how the clay should *not* be modelled.

Fig. 40: Form the basic features by pressing and pulling the clay with your fingers. Alter the position and size of these in the plastic clay until you are satisfied that they produce the effect you want. The character of the mask is largely formed at this stage, so take time over it and be sure you have got it right before you go on. Care must still be taken to avoid undercuts — see the section.

Fig. 41

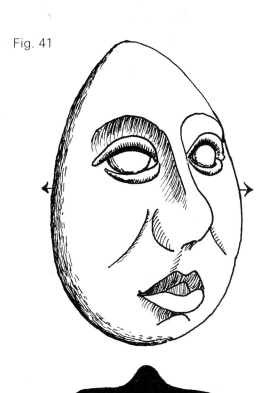

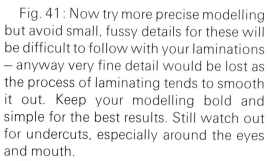

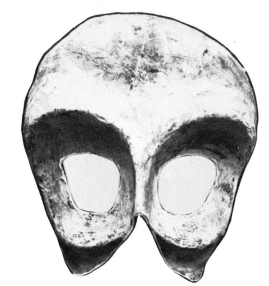

Half-face mask made on clay mould

Paper mask made on clay mould

Fig. 41: Now try more precise modelling but avoid small, fussy details for these will be difficult to follow with your laminations — anyway very fine detail would be lost as the process of laminating tends to smooth it out. Keep your modelling bold and simple for the best results. Still watch out for undercuts, especially around the eyes and mouth.

The photograph on page 27 shows a completed clay mould for a face mask and in colour plate 21 (between pages 36 and 37) you can see three masks which were made on it, but finished in different ways.

Fig. 42

Fig. 43

Figs. 42 and 43 show a mask which fits on top of your head. This is very useful to wear in a play as it leaves your face clear and does not muffle your voice if you are speaking or singing.

Fig. 42 shows the clay mould for a mask of this sort — again be careful about undercuts. A cloth hood can be made to fasten it onto your head, as shown in Fig. 43.

The photograph on page 28 shows a clay mould for an over-head dragon mask and the finished mask is illustrated in colour plate 18 (between pages 36 and 37).

When the modelling is complete, moulds made of modelling clay must be put aside to dry but work can go ahead immediately on a Plasticine mould.

MAKING THE LAMINATED PAPER CASTING

You will need:

Newspaper – in strips 2–3cm (1–1½in) wide
Wallpaper paste or PVA medium
Paste brush
Liquid soap or Vaseline
Craft knife

To make the paper casting easy to remove, smear a fairly generous coat of liquid soap or Vaseline onto the mould. If this soaks into the surface of dry modelling clay, give another coating so that the clay surface stays slightly slippery to the touch.

Paper mask from a clay mould finished with metallic paint

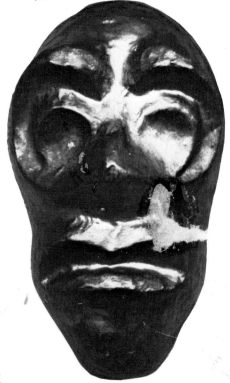

Brush paste generously over the surface of the mould and onto this lay paper strips, brushing them to fit the contours of the mould with a paste-filled brush.

Where the modelling is fairly complex, for example round the eyes and mouth, use narrower strips so that the curves can be followed without wrinkles appearing.

Cover with four to six layers of paper, depending on the size of the mould and how strong it needs to be; for a mask of head size, four are normally enough. Give the final layer a good coating of paste after completion and set the whole thing aside to dry.

When the paper layers are hard, cut round the edge of the mask with a craft knife to release the paper from the base board and ease the paper casting away from the mould. It is now ready for decoration.

You may wish to make a casting to cover only the top half of your face so that your mouth remains clear for speaking. You could make a special mould for this or you could simply laminate paper onto the top part only of a full face mask.

FELT MASKS

Other materials as well as paper can be used to make castings on clay moulds. Strips of cloth are suitable, or pieces of felt. For this the mould must be fairly simple in shape and modelling.

Soak the felt in wallpaper paste or hot decorators' size, lay it over the mould and gradually work it onto the contours, using a stiff brush with a stippling action.

Felt mask from a clay mould

Once the felt has dried and become hard, trim away the surplus with a craft knife and remove the mask from the mould.

Then add any extra features required, using balsa wood, scrap materials, cardboard, string, etc., as in Figs. 44—46 for example. The horns and tusks in Figs. 44 and 45 need to be fixed in place using strips of pasted paper.

MASKS WITH A CARDBOARD BACKING

Give a mask a more impressive appearance by fixing a sheet of thick card to the back of it, with a cut-out in the card to fit your face.

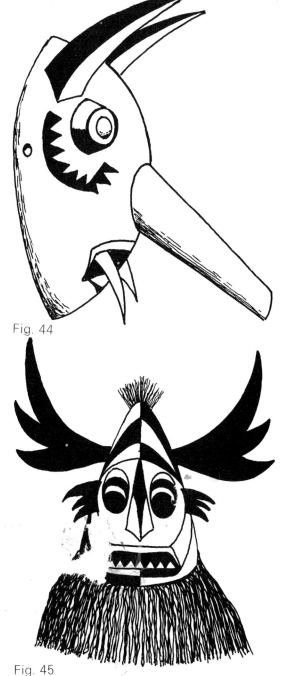

Fig. 44

Fig. 45

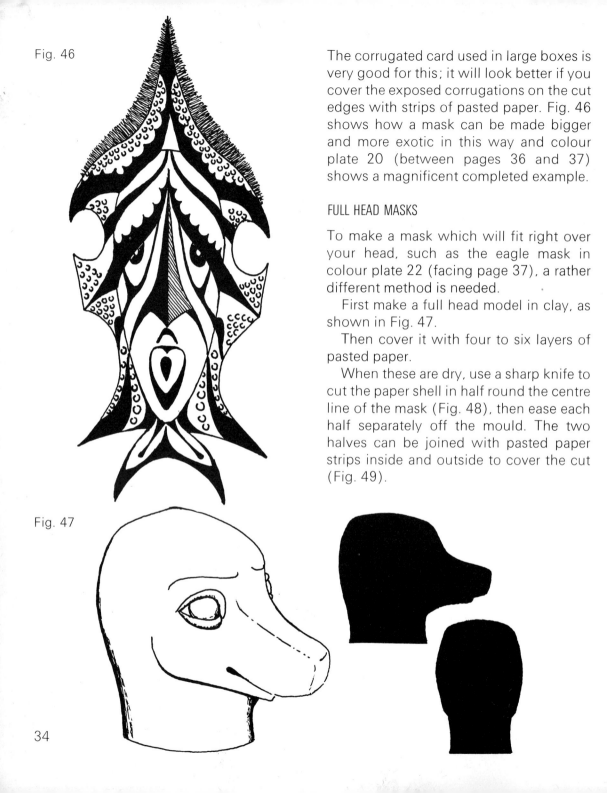

Fig. 46

The corrugated card used in large boxes is very good for this; it will look better if you cover the exposed corrugations on the cut edges with strips of pasted paper. Fig. 46 shows how a mask can be made bigger and more exotic in this way and colour plate 20 (between pages 36 and 37) shows a magnificent completed example.

FULL HEAD MASKS

To make a mask which will fit right over your head, such as the eagle mask in colour plate 22 (facing page 37), a rather different method is needed.

First make a full head model in clay, as shown in Fig. 47.

Then cover it with four to six layers of pasted paper.

When these are dry, use a sharp knife to cut the paper shell in half round the centre line of the mask (Fig. 48), then ease each half separately off the mould. The two halves can be joined with pasted paper strips inside and outside to cover the cut (Fig. 49).

Fig. 47

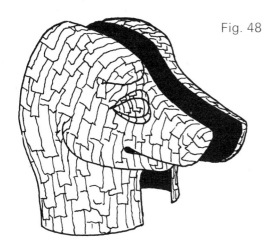
Fig. 48

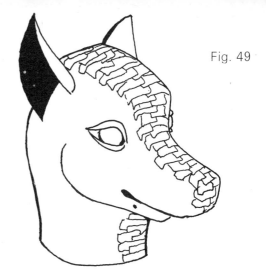
Fig. 49

Decorating and painting

Painting is of course most important. Remember to use the features and contours of your mask as starting points on which to build patterns with decorations or colour. Try to make each colour express the character you want your mask to have. The colour plates may help to give you ideas.

Metallic paints are very useful for de- corating this kind of mask, as shown in colour plate 20 (between pages 36 and 37).

Another technique is to cover the mask with aluminium cooking foil, not worrying about wrinkles but pressing them down flat. PVA medium will hold the foil in position and an interesting finish is given by polishing the surface with black shoe polish, as in colour plate 19 (between pages 36 and 37).

Clay mould for eagle mask

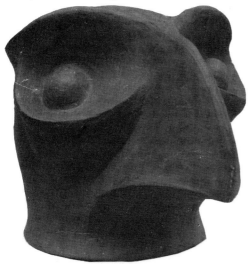

The mould covered in paper strips

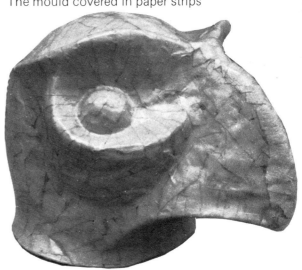

Masks Made On Frames

Another way of making masks, using a wire frame covered with paper laminations, is especially useful for large masks or for single models where you do not want to make identical repeat masks.

The frame can be made of wire or of cane — the kind used for basket weaving. For very large masks, such as carnival "big heads", use wire netting, supported if necessary by a light wooden inner frame which can be removed after the mask is completed. Here we shall be concerned with wire frame making, but the same principles can be applied to other materials.

Wire

The most suitable wire is the galvanised sort which can be bought by weight from ironmongers and is sometimes available as waste from packaging. This bends easily, keeps its shape and is not difficult to cut.

Wire is obtainable in a range of thicknesses or gauges and the larger the mask, the heavier the wire should be. Sixteen and twenty gauge wire is suitable for average sized masks.

Soft, thin florists' wire, also available from ironmongers, is useful for binding joints.

The number of wires to be used will vary according to the size of the mask. The frames shown in Figs. 54–56 would be suitable for masks of about head size. Bigger ones would need a larger number of wires.

CARD AND WIRE FRAMES

Figs. 50–52 show one way of starting to make a wire frame mask, using a cardboard base onto which the frame is built.

Paper mask on card and wire frame

You will need:

Cardboard — packing boxes are suitable as they have an inner corrugated layer into which wire ends can be pushed and glued in position

13. (*Above right*) Wire frame mask with ball castings added

14. (*Above left*) Animal mask on wire frame

15. Bird mask on card and wire frame

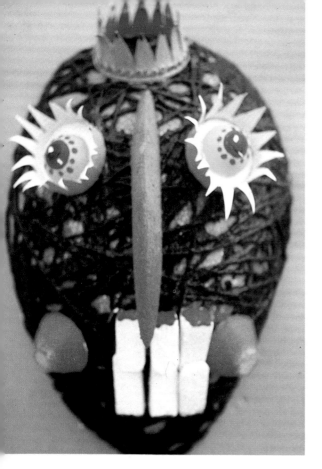

16. (*Above left*)
Balloon casting
made of plaster-
soaked string

17. (*Above right*)
Laminated paper
casting from clay
mould

18. Over-head
dragon mask from
clay mould

19. (*Above left*) Laminated paper casting covered with cooking foil

20. (*Above right*) Paper casting from a clay mould with a backing of strong card, decorated with metallic paint and pasta

21. Three paper masks from the same mould

22. Completed eagle mask

23. (*Below left*) Mask made from waste cut off balloon casting

24. (*Below right*) Mould made from life with plaster bandages. Casting made from the mould (*below*)

Fairly thick wire (see above) — for basic
  frame
Thinner wire — for supporting network
Soft florists' wire — for binding joints
Wire cutters

Cut the card into whatever shape you
require, with an inner cut-out to fit over
your face or on top of your head (see Figs.
50–52).

Cut the main wire frame members to
size, bend into shape and glue in place
with their ends pushed into the card. The
figures show how this is done for different
styles of mask.

When two wires have to be joined, wind
one round the other in a spiral. Be careful
not to leave sharp wire ends sticking out as
these could be dangerous when wearing
the mask.

Fig. 50

Fig. 51

Fig. 52

37

Try to keep ends lying parallel with the main wires and if necessary bind them into place with soft wire. You can also put extra layers of paper covering over joins.

Once the main members of the frame are fixed, build up a supporting network of thinner wires. Secure these in position with soft florists' wire (see Figs. 50–56).

WIRE FRAMES

Figs. 53–56 show wire frames without a cardboard base. These can be made in various shapes but they all start with the basic oval shown in Fig 53. As this is the main bearer on which the other wires will be fastened, be careful to make it the

Fig. 53

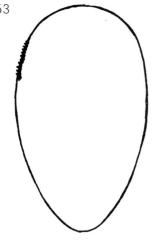

Fig. 54

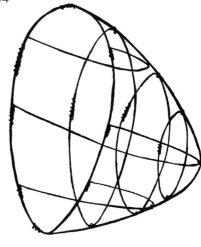

Fig. 55

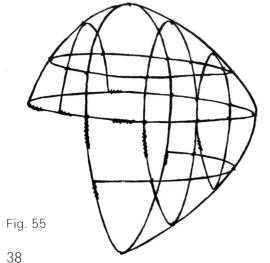

Fig. 56

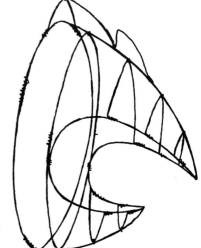

right size and shape to fit over your face.

Remember also that the paper covering will make the opening slightly smaller, so this must be allowed for when making the shape.

Once the basic shape is ready, add the other wires and hold in position by twisting round the ends. Tie with soft wire at points where wires cross.

The frame in Fig. 56 would make a mask like that in the photograph on page 40 — ideal for use in drama as the opening in the front allows unobstructed speech. The masks shown in Figs. 57 and 60 would also be useful for this purpose.

There are many other shapes you can make with wire frames; Figs. 58 and 59 are just two more examples.

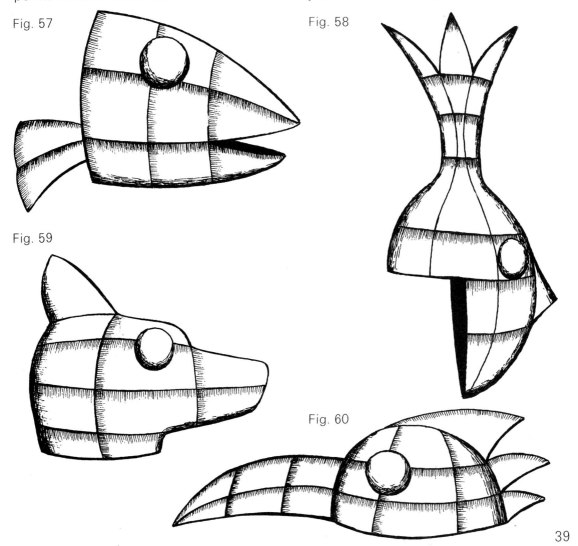

Fig. 57

Fig. 58

Fig. 59

Fig. 60

As you work on the frame, check it continuously for symmetry by examining it from different angles. Wires which become distorted can easily be put right provided the fault is noticed soon enough. It becomes much more difficult to correct a shape or curve if work goes on and other wires are attached to the faulty one.

MAKING THE LAMINATED PAPER COVERING

Simply place strips of paste-soaked paper across the wires, at first lapping them over onto their own inner surfaces to hold them in place. Because the frame contributes greatly to the strength of the mask, use only two or three layers of paper.

Make the junction of the cardboard support and the wire frame smooth by running strips of paper from the frame onto the card and adjusting them to give a curved join.

Take care that all the ends and edges of the strips are well brushed down, avoiding gaps and wrinkles. As the paste in the paper dries, it will shrink the paper and make it taut, providing a good surface to paint on.

When the mask is dry, use scrap materials, card shapes, paper castings from balls etc. to create features and finally paint it.

Colour plates 13 and 14 (facing page 36) show two completed masks.

CLOTH MASKS

Materials other than paper may be used to cover wire frames. Strips of paste-soaked cloth are one alternative and with these only one layer is needed. Plaster impregnated surgical bandages are another possible covering. They make a rather heavier mask but it has an interestingly textured surface. If the covering is coated both inside and out with PVA medium, this will prevent the plaster flaking off.

Fitting

Because the rim of masks with wire frames is often uneven and can be uncomfortable when worn, it is worthwhile sticking on a strip of heavy cloth, such as velvet or corduroy, after the mask is painted. Straps to hold the mask in position can be made of the same material.

Make eye holes in suitable positions. They need not be large and splitting or tearing of the covering can be prevented by sticking small strips of cloth or heavy paper round the edges of the holes on the inside of the mask.

Plaster bandages on wire-framed bird mask

Repeat Masks – Paper And Plaster

If a large number of masks has to be made to one design, or if you want to keep your design in a more lasting form than the original clay model, which is easily broken or chipped with frequent use, it is worthwhile making a plaster cast. As well as being more durable, this gives an exact replica of the original as it produces a negative mould and details do not become blurred by the thickness of the paper laminations.

Fig. 61

MAKING A MOULD

You will need:

Clay
Modelling board
Strips of plywood or hardboard; lino or
vinyl can also be used and will follow
the shape of the material, using less
plaster
Masking tape
Plaster of Paris
Plastic bowl or bucket

Fig. 62

First make a clay original on a modelling board, as described on page 28 (see also Fig. 61). Undercuts must again be avoided. Do not let the clay dry.

Fig. 62 shows how to make a moulding box around your model, using the plywood/hardboard or lino/vinyl.

The joins in the moulding box must be sealed carefully with masking tape and the joints with the base board closed with clay (see Fig. 62). Be very sure the seals are secure so that liquid plaster cannot escape.

Mix your plaster by adding Plaster of Paris slowly to cold water in a plastic bowl or bucket and stirring gently until you get a smooth, creamy liquid.

Without delay, as plaster sets quite quickly, pour the plaster over the model until its highest point is covered by about 2cm (1in).

Once the plaster has set, remove the moulding box, turn over the casting and take out the clay original.

Allow the plaster mould to dry thoroughly in a warm place.

MAKING THE LAMINATED PAPER SHELL

Coat the surface of the mould with liquid soap or Vaseline. Several coats may be needed as the first layers will soak into the plaster.

When the surface is slightly slippery, brush paste-soaked paper strips inside it (Fig. 63) and build them up to 4–6 layers. Remove when dry and hard.

Trim the edges and the mask is ready for painting.

The mould can be re-used immediately though it may need a further coat of liquid soap or Vaseline.

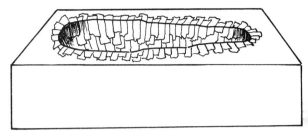

Fig. 63

Plaster mould for repeat castings

Repeat Masks – Glass Reinforced Plastics

Extremely durable moulds and masks can be made using polyester resins and glass fibre. Such a mould may be used for making large numbers of masks of laminated paper, cloth or felt, or masks which are themselves made of glass reinforced plastics. Plastic masks are very strong but rather heavy and rigid to wear. They are perhaps most suitable for wall hanging.

Resins should be used with great caution as the materials are inflammable and can irritate some skins:

Work in a large, well ventilated space and away from naked flames
Coat your hands with barrier cream before starting work and clean them with cleansing cream as soon as you have finished

Be careful not to splash catalyst about
Clean brushes and other tools as soon as you can.

For mould and mask making you will need:

Clay for the original model
Pre-activated Gelcoat resin
Pre-activated lay-up resin
Glass fibre mat (42 grams – $1\frac{1}{2}$ oz)
Catalyst
Wax polish containing no silicones
Waxed paper cups
2cm (1in) wide brushes
Barrier cream to protect hands while working
Hand cleansing cream
Brush cleaner

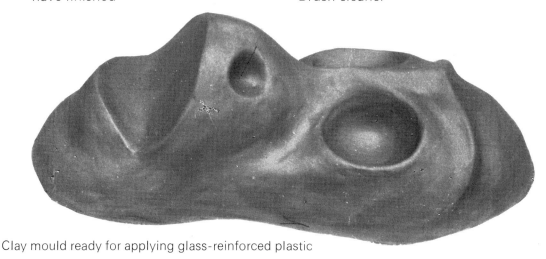

Clay mould ready for applying glass-reinforced plastic

(A number of firms specialise in the supply of these materials, which are available in small quantities for craft purposes. Two of the best known are: Tiranti's, Goodge Place, London WC1, and Trylon, Thrift St, Wollaston, Northants.)

Make a clay model on a base board as described on page 28. Again, avoid under-cuts.

When the model is complete (Fig. 64), allow it to become leather-hard, that is firm to the touch and free of moisture on the surface, but not completely dried out. Casting can be carried out when the clay is completely dry but the cast is then much more difficult to remove from the mould later.

Add 2 per cent of catalyst to gelcoat resin in a waxed paper cup, mix thoroughly and brush generously onto the model and a 2cm (1in) wide surround of the base board (Fig. 65). This becomes tacky to the touch in about 20–30 minutes and it is then ready for lay-up resin and glass fibre to be applied.

Fig. 64

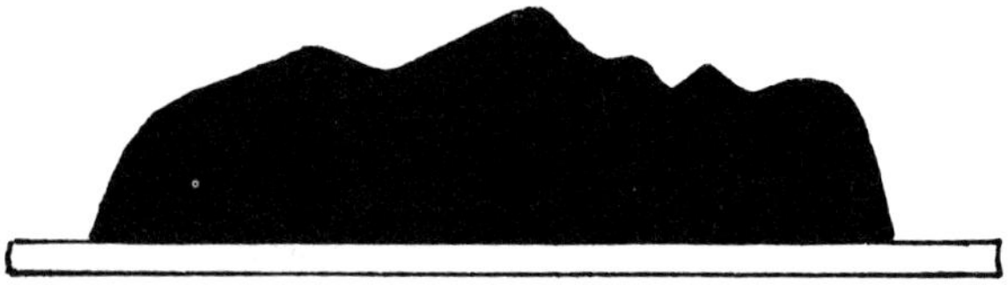

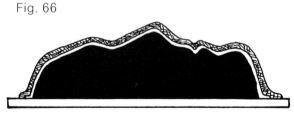

clay model

Fig. 65

gel coat

Fig. 66

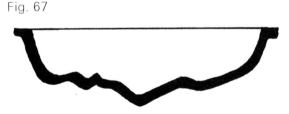

resin and glass fibre

Fig. 67

clay removed, mould waxed

Cut a piece of glass fibre mat a little larger than the model and mix 2 per cent of catalyst with lay-up resin.

Brush a generous coat of resin on top of the gelcoat and place the glass fibre over it.

Mould the glass fibre to the contours of the model by using a brush with a dabbing or stippling motion. Gradually you will find that the glass fibre mat becomes impregnated with resin and takes on the shape of the mask (Fig. 66).

Be sure to eliminate air bubbles by working on them with the brush, pushing them out to the edges of the glass mat.

A second layer of glass fibre should now be put on.

After about 20–30 minutes, the resin will set to a jelly-like hardness. Trim the surplus glass fibre and resin away with a sharp knife. Leave the resin to cure overnight and the next day the mould can be prised off the base board and the clay model removed (Fig. 67).

Wash all traces of clay out of the mould, then polish the inside surface thoroughly with wax polish containing no silicones.

The mould may now be used for making paper, cloth or felt castings, as with a plaster mould (see page 32), or for making plastic castings. Here the process is the same as for making the mould, but now working on the mould's inside surface.

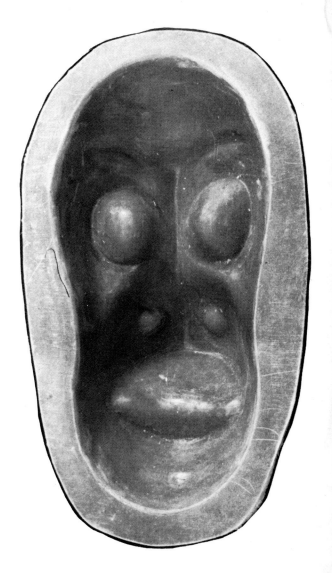

Finished plastic mould for repeat castings

Fig. 68

Fig. 69

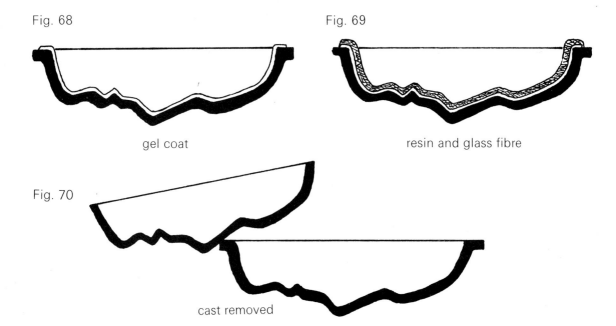

gel coat

resin and glass fibre

Fig. 70

cast removed

MAKING A PLASTIC CASTING

Apply the catalysed gelcoat to the inside of the mould (Fig. 68).

Apply two layers of catalysed lay-up resin and glass fibre mat (see page 45 and Fig. 69).

Allow to gel and then trim off the surplus with a knife.

After the resin has cured, remove the cast from the mould (Fig. 70).

Pigments for colouring your mask can be added to the resin before moulding or applied, mixed with resin and catalyst, to the completed casting.

Modelling Masks From Life

It is quite easy to produce a mask which is an exact copy of someone's face by making a plaster mould directly onto it.

MAKING THE MOULD

It is important to have all your materials close at hand as you will have to work quickly once you start.

You will need:

A 5cm (2in) roll of plaster impregnated
   surgical bandage
Bowl of water
Scissors
Vaseline

Cut bandage into pieces 8cm (3in) long.

Get your model comfortably seated and warn him or her that, once you start, sneezing, coughing, nose blowing or movement of face muscles will spoil the mould.

Rub Vaseline on to the face, smoothing eyebrows down well with a generous coating. (Avoid moustaches or beards!)

Make sure that the hair is out of the way and tied back if necessary. Ask the model to close his mouth lightly and to breathe through his nose.

Dip pieces of bandage into the water, shake off the surplus, and press them gently over the contours of the face. Work round the eyes carefully and keep the nostrils clear. Carry on until the whole face is covered, except for eyes and nostrils, by two complete layers.

Leave the plaster to set, which will take only a few minutes, then gently ease the mould away from the face.

Trim the edges of the mould; do any patching or neatening that is needed around the eyes and nostrils with more plaster bandage applied to the outside of the mould.

MAKING A CAST

If you want to make several casts from the mould, strengthen it with one or two additional layers of bandage on the outside.

To make the cast, use either two more layers of plaster bandage or layers of paper strips, soaked with paste.

Smear the *inside* of the mould with Vaseline or liquid soap.

Press the layers of plaster bandage onto the inside surface of the mould, or build up layers of paper strips as described for the plaster mould on page 42.

When these have set, ease them out of the mould and trim the edges of the cast. A plaster bandage mould with a cast taken from it, is shown in colour plate 24 (facing page 37), but you might like to paint yours to make it look more realistic.

Conclusion

Remember that techniques are only a means to an end — ways of transforming your ideas into solid objects. Knowledge of techniques gives you a starting point to develop away from, towards experimenting with your own personal ways of using materials to make something which is unique, your own creation.

Do try out your own ideas for using materials. There are no hard and fast rules to say that particular ways of doing things are right and others are wrong. What counts is whether the way *you* do it produces the result that *you* want.

Of course you will have disappointments and failures but it is worthwhile discovering the limitations of techniques and materials as well as their possibilities, if you use your new knowledge and experience positively to increase your skill.

The world around you is a welter of different colours and shapes; people, places and things can all provide inspiration — keep your eyes open and you will never be short of ideas for your masks.